W9-CKH-231

XTREME ROBOTS

Rescue Robots

S.L. HAMILTON

A&D Xtreme
An imprint of Abdo Publishing | abdobooks.com

abdobooks.com

Published by Abdo Publishing, a division of ABDO, PO Box 398166, Minneapolis, Minnesota 55439.

Printed in the United States of America, North Mankato, MN.
092018
012019

Editor: John Hamilton
Copy Editor: Bridget O'Brien
Graphic Design: Sue Hamilton
Cover Design: Candice Keimig and Pakou Moua
Cover Photo: Dreamstime
Interior Photos & Illustrations: AirRobot-pg 20 (top); Alamy-pgs 18-19, 21 & 32; AP-pgs 1 & 10-11; ASV Global-pgs 2-3; Carnegie Mellon University-pgs 8 & 9; Dreamstime-pgs 4-5; Getty-pgs 28-29; Harvard University-pgs 12 & 13; Hydronalix-pgs 22 & 23; iStock-pgs 20 (bottom), 21 (inset) & 30-31; NATO Centre for Maritime Research and Experimentation (CMRE)/ICARUS European Project-pgs 26 & 27; Örebro University-pg 16; QinetiQ North America-pgs 6 & 7; Russian Defence Ministry-pg 19; Sandia National Labs-pg 14; Science Source-pgs 17 & 24-25; U.S. Army-pg 15 (bottom); U.S. Marines-pg 15 (top); Wikimedia-pg 17 (top inset).

Library of Congress Control Number: 2018949994
Publisher's Cataloging-in-Publication Data

Names: Hamilton, S.L., author.
Title: Rescue robots / by S.L. Hamilton.
Description: Minneapolis, Minnesota : Abdo Publishing, 2019 | Series: Xtreme robots | Includes online resources and index.
Identifiers: ISBN 9781532118272 (lib. bdg.) | ISBN 9781532171451 (ebook)
Subjects: LCSH: Robots in search and rescue operations--Juvenile literature. | Disaster robotics--Juvenile literature. | Robots--Juvenile literature. | Robotics--Juvenile literature.
Classification: DDC 629.892--dc23

Contents

Rescue Robots

Rescue robots go where there is extreme danger to humans. They are used at fires, floods, earthquakes, avalanches, and even nuclear disasters. Some are big enough to carry gallons of water or injured people. Others are small enough to search spaces where victims might be trapped. Rescue robots roll, crawl, fly, and swim to help people.

XTREME FACT – The first known use of rescue robots was in September 2001 when New York's World Trade Center collapsed after terrorist-flown jets struck and destroyed the Twin Towers.

Early Rescue Robots

Early robotics pioneers quickly realized that their work could help with search and rescue (SAR). SAR first responders often risk their lives. They go into collapsed buildings, tunnels, caves, and mines. They face smoke and fire. They take on dangerous water. Sometimes they can't reach people in trouble. Robots can help.

First responders use a rescue robot to search through rubble at New York's World Trade Center disaster in 2001.

In September 2001, a Talon search and rescue robot was sent into a rubble-filled area of one of the World Trade Center's basement areas in hopes of finding survivors.

Robots can go into places where first responders and search dogs may be in extreme danger. Robots can go into small places. They can go into "hot spots." They can search through rubble and survive falls. They can "see" if a human is trapped or if no one is there. Early rescue robots were wired with a human operator. Many of today's robots are wireless. Some even operate by themselves. This is called being autonomous. Robots are excellent assistants.

XTREME QUOTE – "Responders expect to continue to risk their lives to save others; robots don't replace their rapid actions or sacrifices but rather eliminate unnecessary risks." –Robin Murphy, **Disaster Robotics**

Underground SAR Robots

Snakebot is small and flexible. It is designed to go nto collapsed buildings and other structures. Called a peek robot," it has a lighted front camera that sends video to rescuers on the surface. Rescuers are able to see where people may be trapped after an earthquake or other disaster.

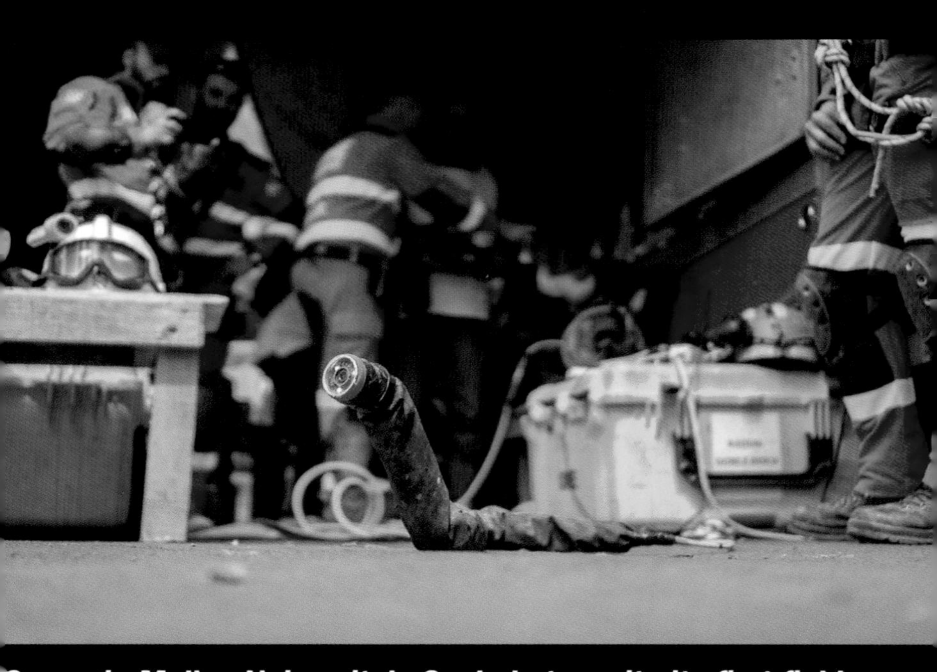

Carnegie Mellon University's Snakebot awaits its first field use

Snakebot is prepared to enter a collapsed building in Mexico. Its job was to look for people who had not been heard from since the earthquake.

Snakebot is 2 inches (5 cm) in diameter and 37 inches (94 cm) long. It is made of connected joints that allow it to move forward and backward, climb up and down, and even roll across debris.

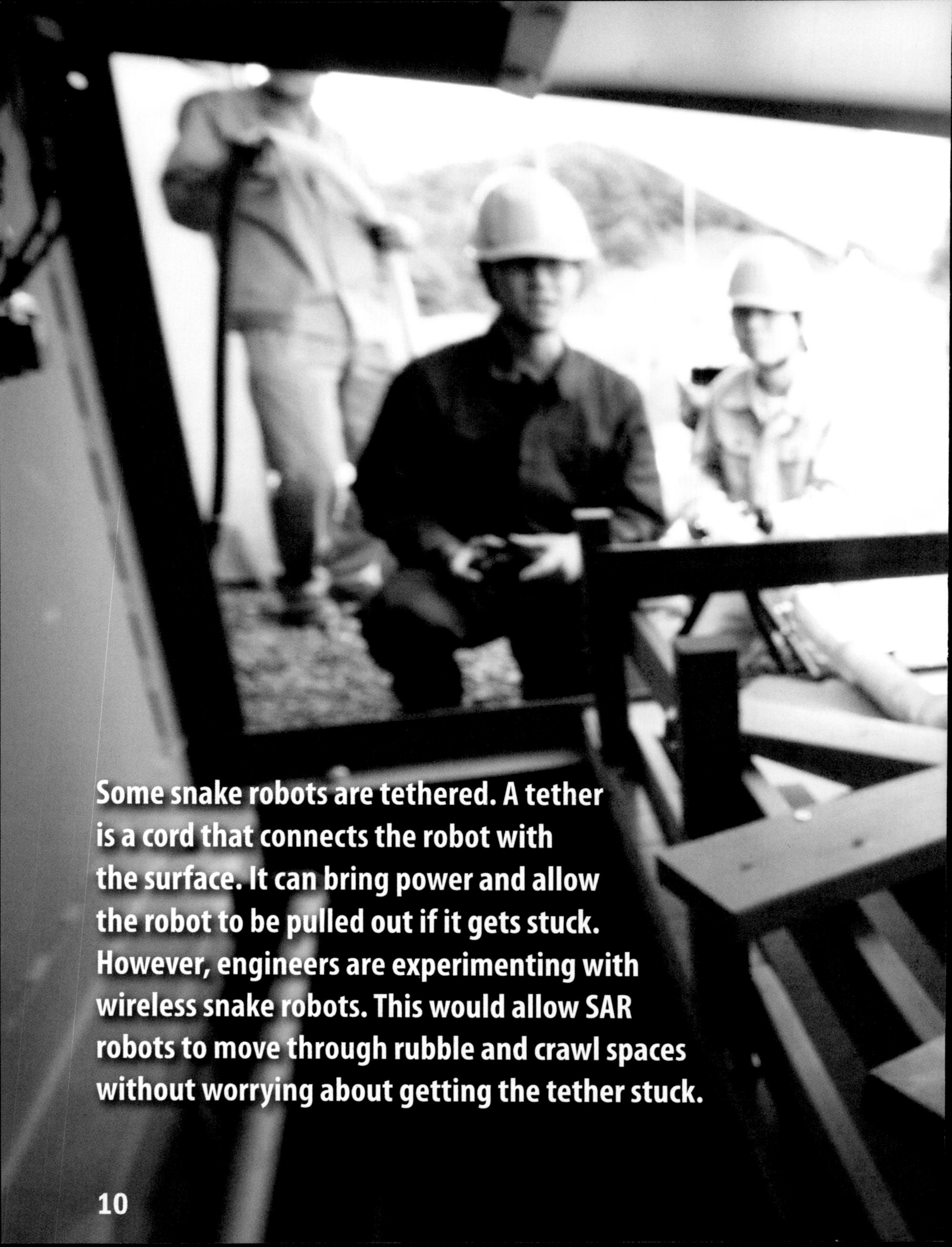

Some snake robots are tethered. A tether is a cord that connects the robot with the surface. It can bring power and allow the robot to be pulled out if it gets stuck. However, engineers are experimenting with wireless snake robots. This would allow SAR robots to move through rubble and crawl spaces without worrying about getting the tether stuck.

Japan's Tohoku University created a snake robot that can go into pipes and through rubble.

XTREME FACT – Future snake search and rescue robots may be equipped with microphones and speakers so people who are trapped can talk and listen to rescuers on the surface.

Harvard University has developed a cockroach-sized robot that can easily fit into small, enclosed spaces. It is called HAMR, or Harvard Ambulatory MicroRobot. It weighs about the same as a United States penny and is less than 1.8 inches (4.5 cm) long. It is also *fast*. The scuttling bug-like robot moves across the ground at a rate of about four body lengths per second. But HAMR is not limited to running across a floor. Fitted with special footpads, it can also move on top of water and dive under the surface.

HAMR's special footpads let it walk on water.

HAMR

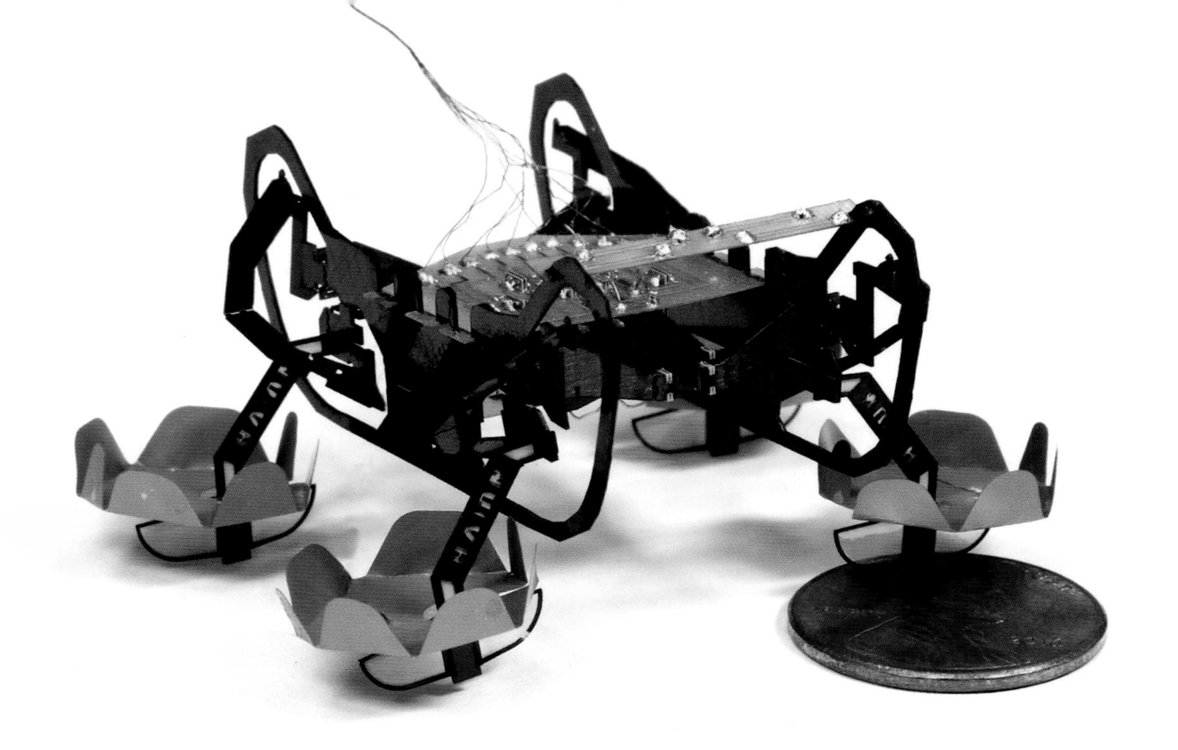

Just like its cockroach counterpart, HAMR can run, climb, and jump. Because it is so lightweight, if it falls it is not damaged. For search-and-rescue jobs, it can go into areas that are radioactive or filled with poisonous gases. Engineers have worked to make it autonomous so it could move by itself into very small places underground. There is one problem. Would trapped people be happy to see it or would they squish it?

XTREME FACT – Only about 20% of disaster survivors are rescued from inside destroyed structures. Eighty percent of survivors are on, or can be seen from, the surface.

Mine disasters present many challenges. Besides piles of rubble, there may be poisonous gases, standing water, and unstable walls and ceilings. Sandia National Labs has created the Gemini-Scout Mine Rescue Robot to aid first responders. The robot's pan-and-tilt cameras scan entire areas. Its tires allow it to move over rubble and through 18 inches (46 cm) of water. It is even equipped with gas sensors and a thermal camera to locate survivors.

Gemini-Scout Mine Rescue Robot

Talon has enough power to pull a victim out of danger.

Talon is a robot designed to go into dangerous situations. Produced by QinetiQ North America, it was first used in search and rescue at the World Trade Center disaster in 2001. It is highly mobile. It can travel over rocks and roug terrain. It can move through water and mud. It can lift an move heavy objects. Its camera sends images to a ground operator, who can look for hurt and injured people.

Talon can maneuver down stairs.

Smoke & Fire Robots

Smokebot

Dangerous situations are even more life-threatening when first responders can't see what's ahead of them. Smokebot can go into smoky, foggy, dusty, and even fire-filled areas. It uses cameras, radar, laser scanners, and gas sensors to give emergency workers a map of what they are facing. This allows them to make an action plan from a safe distance.

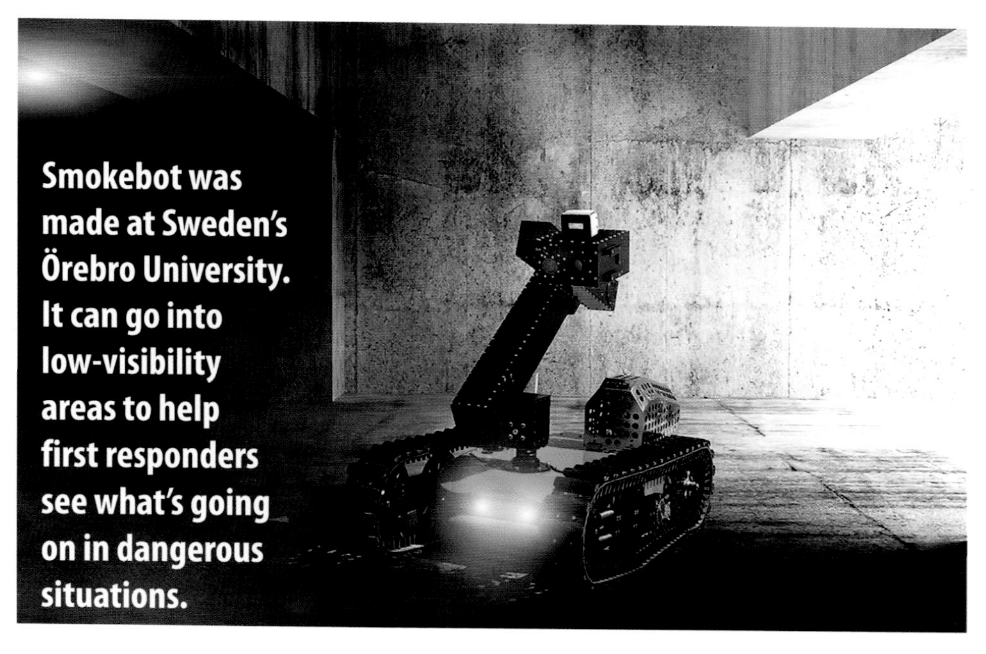
Smokebot was made at Sweden's Örebro University. It can go into low-visibility areas to help first responders see what's going on in dangerous situations.

Shrewbot is another robot designed to help firefighters and other first responders who must go into emergency situations where there is no light. Shrewbot is a biomimicry robot based on the Etruscan pygmy shrew. Like the tiny rodent, Shrewbot uses 18 extended whiskers to feel its way through dark areas.
It can map its surroundings and send the information to operators. The whiskers may one day work like fingers. They could touch a surface and feel shapes, textures, and temperature.

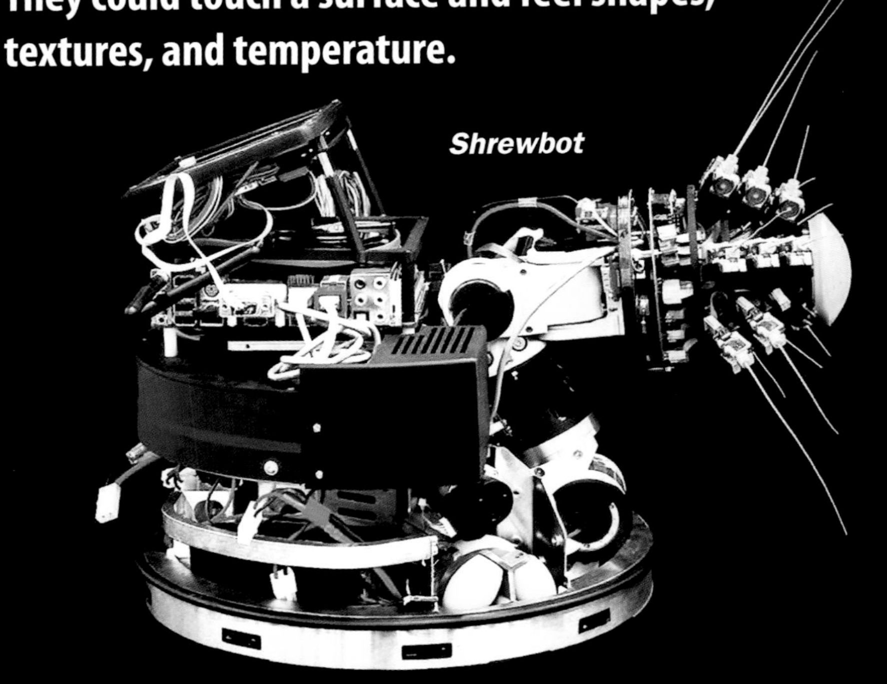
Shrewbot

XTREME FACT – Some rescue robots are fitted with carbon dioxide detectors that can tell if there is a person nearby and if they are breathing.

The Russian Defence Ministry's Uran-14 is a UGV (unmanned ground vehicle) designed for fighting fires in remote areas and large warehouses. It has a tank base with a front bulldozer blade and tong-like grippers that can clear debris.

Uran-14 UGV holds 528 gallons of water (2,000 liters) or 132 gallons (500 liters) of foam. Two operators control the Uran-14's sensors and movements. It has serious firefighting abilities.

Additional water tanks can be mounted to the outside of the Uran-14. It can shoot water in all directions.

The UGV's front grippers and blade can cut through debris and clear obstacles.

Aerial SAR Robots

An eye-in-the-sky is a great advantage to search and rescue workers. UAVs (unmanned aerial vehicles) are camera-equipped drones. Most carry a video camera, but some have a still or infrared camera. These robotic observers can fly in all directions or hover in place. UAVs may be used to search for people lost in the wilderness or missing after a natural disaster, such as an earthquake or flood. They may also be used inside buildings, such as during a fire or nuclear disaster.

UAVs are also known as UASs (unmanned aerial systems) and RPVs (remotely piloted vehicles). All of these drones have a human pilot operating them.

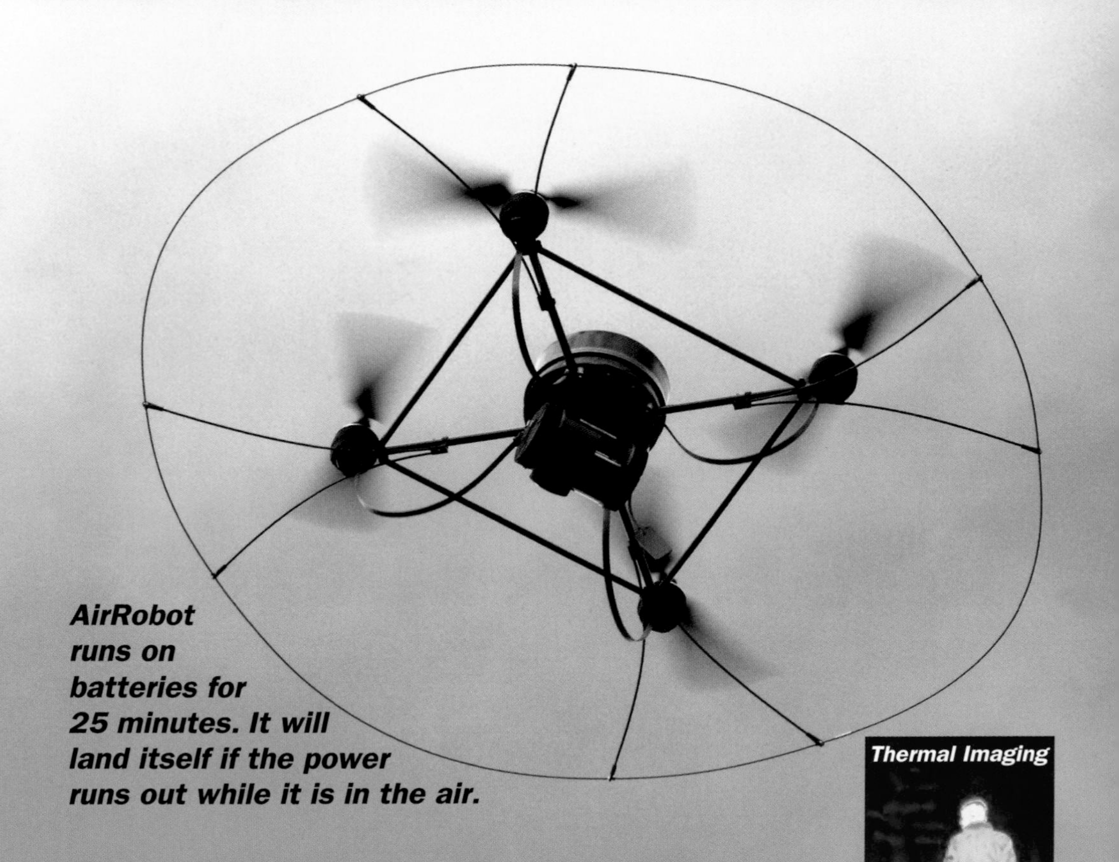

AirRobot runs on batteries for 25 minutes. It will land itself if the power runs out while it is in the air.

AirRobot is a micro UAV that can fly day or night. It has video and thermal imaging cameras. A first responder uses the airborne drone to search and observe. It is launched in less than a minute and flown by a single operator. The video feed lets a pilot feel as though he or she are flying along with it. AirRobot can go as far away as 1,800 feet (549 m) and as high as 3,000 feet (914 m). It flies at a speed of 25 miles per hour (40 kph), but can also hover in place. This gives search and rescue workers time to look carefully around an area.

Water Rescue Robots

Unmanned marine vehicles (UMV) may operate above or below the water's surface. They are robots created to assist in water rescues. Some help tired or injured swimmers on the surface. Others go deep to assist trapped submarine personnel or workers in underwater oil and gas structures.

XTREME FACT – UMVs work in either deep water or littoral environments. Littoral is the shallower areas near the shore and by piers, bridges, and marinas.

EMILY is a lifesaving robot designed to race across the water's surface to help victims.

EMILY is a 4-foot (1-m) -long robotic buoy that can support up to five people.

EMILY is an unmanned surface vehicle (USV). EMILY stands for Emergency Integrated Lifesaving Lanyard. It is a remote-controlled floatation device with speed. The robotic USV can travel through wild water at a speed of 30 miles per hour (48 kph). It does not have a propeller, but uses a jet pump to move. It can be placed in the water at the shore, or dropped from a boat, plane, or helicopter. EMILY is used by lifeguards and other SAR workers when people are in trouble and extra time is needed for help to arrive. EMILY can keep up to five people afloat.

Some rescue robots are designed to work underwater. The H1000 ROV (remotely operated vehicle) can travel as deep as .62 miles (1,000 m) to stranded submarines and other underwater stations. Its video cameras can search and locate problems. It has arms and tools to perform work such as clearing debris or repairing electronics on the outside of a ship. It can even deliver

Unmanned surface vehicles (USV) are robotic boats. They are designed to run without a human on board. They may move by themselves (autonomously) or by remote control with a human operator at the helm. Teaming an unmanned aerial vehicle (UAV) with an unmanned surface vehicle (USV) provides the best of both worlds.

One unmanned maritime system being tested is a program called ICARUS (Integrated Components for Assisted Rescue and Unmanned Search Operations). Combining unmanned air and water robots may lead to greater recovery successes.

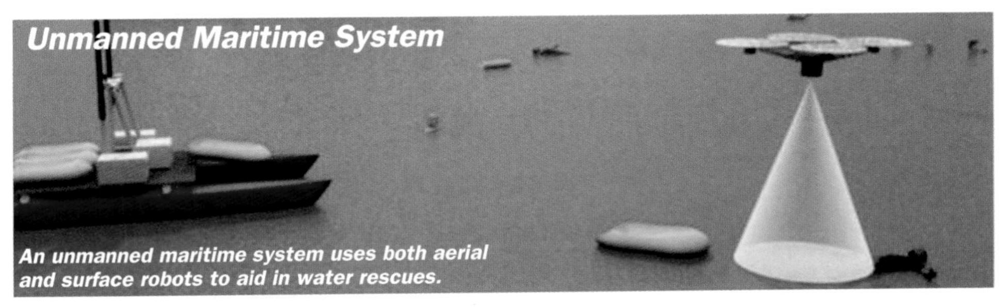
Unmanned Maritime System

An unmanned maritime system uses both aerial and surface robots to aid in water rescues.

A UAV searches for victims from the sky, sending video to the command center.

A USV speeds toward victims in the water.

The USV launches a smaller boat with supplies.

The boat may carry a raft, life preservers, or communication devices.

An unmanned maritime system uses a search and rescue drone's thermal sensors to look for a victim's body heat in cold seawater. Once a person is located, a USV is sent out. The USV may carry a smaller boat that can bring a rescue raft or other supplies to the injured or stranded victims. This allows enough time for search and rescue workers to get to them. Using an entire system of unmanned air and marine vehicles brings greater success to rescue operations.

Nuclear Disaster Robots

Radiation is an ever-present danger near nuclear disaster sites. The health and safety of first responders is at risk. Engineers are working on remotely operated mobile robots that can go into a site to rescue the sick and injured.

A Japanese ROV (remotely operated vehicle) acts as a stretcher. It is able to load a victim onto a ramp, retract the ramp inside the vehicle, and drive the person to safety. Some people who helped test the rescue robot found the experience a bit frightening. The robot does not hurt them, but they said being retracted into the vehicle's body feels like going into a coffin. However, once loaded inside, the victims are carted to safety. If you were hurt, would you mind being rescued by a robot?

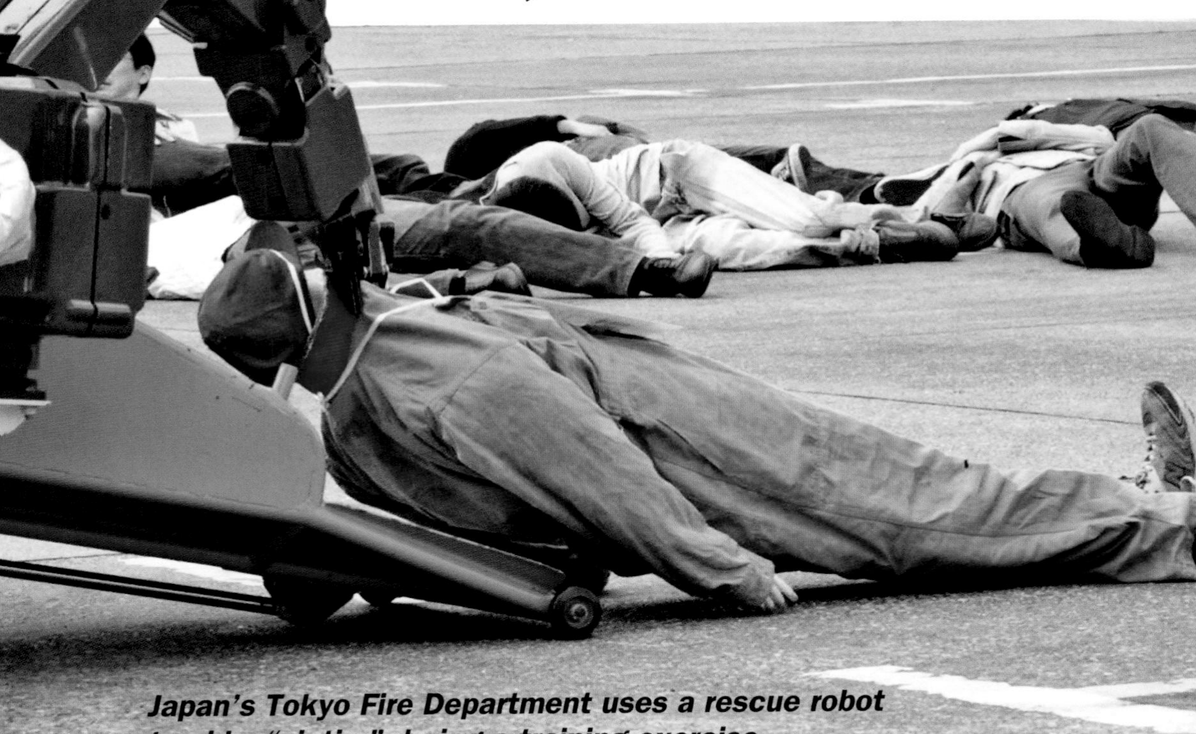

Japan's Tokyo Fire Department uses a rescue robot to aid a "victim" during a training exercise.

Glossary

Autonomous
Able to work on its own. An autonomous robot does not have a human operating it. Its programming allows it to do its job without help.

Biomimicry
When engineers use a life-form in nature to create robots.

Carbon Dioxide
A gas that humans and other mammals give off when they exhale.

Diameter
The measurement of a straight line passing through an object from one side to the other.

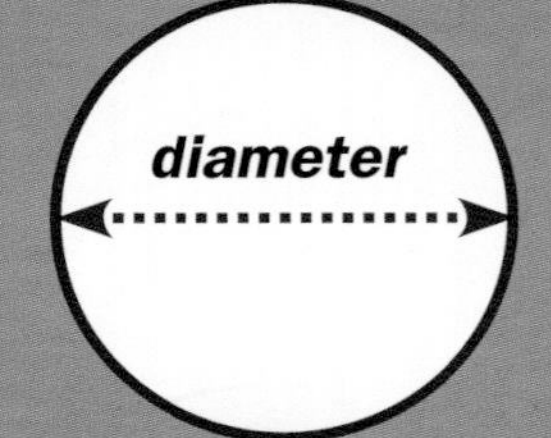

Engineer
A person whose job is to use scientific knowledge to create and maintain mechanical and electronic objects and structures. This includes such things as robots, cameras, and engines.

First Responders
People such as police, firefighters, ambulance drivers, emergency medical technicians (EMTs) and paramedics, who are the first on the scene of an emergency situation.

Hot Spots
A place where the temperature is much hotter than the surrounding area, often caused by fire.

RADIATION
A kind of energy that comes from a radioactive source such as uranium. It can cause sickness or be fatal to people who are exposed.

SEARCH AND RESCUE
Search and rescue (SAR) are teams who find and return to safety people who have survived emergency situations. The teams may be made up of individuals, dogs, and robots.

SENSORS
In robots, devices that send out signals and get information from a surrounding area. The robot's computers may use the data to decide what the robot should do next, or pass the collected information on to a human operator.

TETHER
A connecting rope or wire. In robots, it may be used to keep an object from moving too far away or as a way to get power to the robot.

THERMAL CAMERA
A type of camera that photographs or videotapes the heat given off by something (such as a person) that is warmer than its surroundings.

Online Resources

To learn more about rescue robots, visit abdobooklinks.com. These links are routinely monitored and updated to provide the most current information available.

Index